HANDY HEALTH GUIDE TO BURNS AND BLISTERS

Alvin and Virginia Silverstein
and Laura Silverstein Nunn

Enslow Publishers, Inc.
40 Industrial Road
Box 398
Berkeley Heights, NJ 07922
USA

http://www.enslow.com

Original edition published as *Burns and Blisters* in 2002.

Library of Congress Cataloging-in-Publication Data
Silverstein, Alvin.
Handy health guide to burns and blisters / by Alvin Silverstein, Virginia Silverstein, and Laura Silverstein Nunn.
pages cm. — (Handy health guides)
Includes index.
 ISBN 978-0-7660-4272-8
 1. Burns and scalds—Juvenile literature. 2. Blisters—Juvenile literature. 3. Skin—Wounds and injuries—Juvenile
literature. I. Silverstein, Virginia B. II. Nunn, Laura Silverstein. III. Title. IV. Title: Burns and blisters.
 RD96.4.S546 2014
 617.1'1—dc23
                              2012041449

Future editions:
Paperback ISBN: 978-1-4644-0487-0
EPUB ISBN: 978-1-4645-1252-0
Single-User PDF ISBN: 978-1-4646-1252-7
Multi-User PDF ISBN: 978-0-7660-5884-2

Printed in the United States of America

052013 Lake Book Manufacturing, Inc., Melrose Park, IL

10 9 8 7 6 5 4 3 2 1

To Our Readers: We have done our best to make sure all Internet Addresses in this book were active and appropriate when we went to press. However, the author and the publisher have no control over and assume no liability for the material available on those Internet sites or on other Web sites they may link to. Any comments or suggestions can be sent by e-mail to comments@enslow.com or to the address on the back cover.

♻ Enslow Publishers, Inc., is committed to printing our books on recycled paper. The paper in every book contains 10% to 30% post-consumer waste (PCW). The cover board on the outside of each book contains 100% PCW. Our goal is to do our part to help young people and the environment too!

Illustration Credits: © 2012 Clipart.com, pp. 30, 32; CDC/Dr. Holdeman, p. 35; Comstock/Photos.com, p. 21(top left); David M. Phillips/Photo Researchers, Inc., Colorization by: Mary Martin, p. 14 (bottom); dedMazay/ Photos.com, p. 18; Dr. P. Marazzi/Photo Researchers, Inc., p. 26 (top); Georgios Alexandris/Photos.com, p. 23; intek1/Photos.com, p. 26 (middle, bottom); (c) iStockphoto.com/Paul Kline, p. 41; @ iStockphoto.com/tirc83, p. 21 (bottom); John Takai/Photos.com, p. 43; Juergen Berger/Photo Researchers, Inc., p. 17 (bottom); Jupiterimages/ Photos.com, p. 42; Mike Devlin/Photo Researchers, Inc., pp. 5, 19; Murat Tac/Photos.com, p. 38; Shutterstock.com, pp. 1, 3, 6, 9, 10, 13, 14 (top), 15, 20, 21 (top right), 22, 24, 28, 29, 31, 32, 33, 34, 39; SPL/Photo Researchers, Inc., p. 8; Steve Gschmeissner/Photo Researchers, Inc., p. 17 (top); Thinkstock/Photos.com, p. 4.

Cover Photo: Shutterstock.com (all images)

CONTENTS

Be careful when you are cooking at a hot stove so that you do not get burned.

1
THAT BURNS!

"Hot! Don't touch!" This is probably one of the first warnings your mom or dad gave you. If you were like many little kids, you may not have taken their word for it. You may have accidentally found out the hard way: If you touch a hot stove, you will get burned, and burns can really hurt.

Anybody can get a burn. Burns happen when your skin is damaged by fire, hot objects or liquids, certain chemicals, electricity, or the sun. Most burns are minor and can be treated at home. Serious burns require immediate medical attention or may even mean a stay in the hospital.

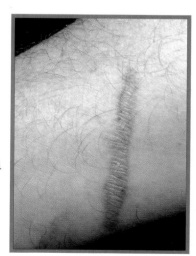

This is a minor burn caused by a hot object.

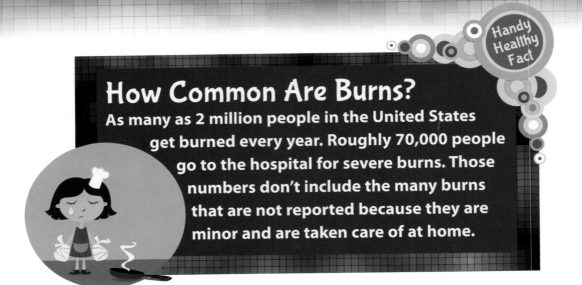

How Common Are Burns?

As many as 2 million people in the United States get burned every year. Roughly 70,000 people go to the hospital for severe burns. Those numbers don't include the many burns that are not reported because they are minor and are taken care of at home.

Some burns are so serious that they may cause lasting health problems, disability, or even death.

Most burns can be prevented. By following some helpful tips, you can reduce your chances of getting burned.

2

THE SKIN YOU LIVE IN

Your body is wrapped in a protective coating—your skin. The skin is the largest organ of the body. It makes up as much as 15 percent of your body weight. Like any other organ of the body, your skin does important jobs that help keep you healthy.

Skin is soft and elastic, but it is strong. It can handle all kinds of wear and tear, and can even repair minor damage. It protects you, keeping dangerous chemicals and most germs from getting inside your body and harming you. At the same time, it keeps fluids inside and protects the body from drying out. Skin helps to keep our temperature constant, cooling us in hot weather and holding in warmth when it is cold outside. The skin is also a sense organ, letting you know about

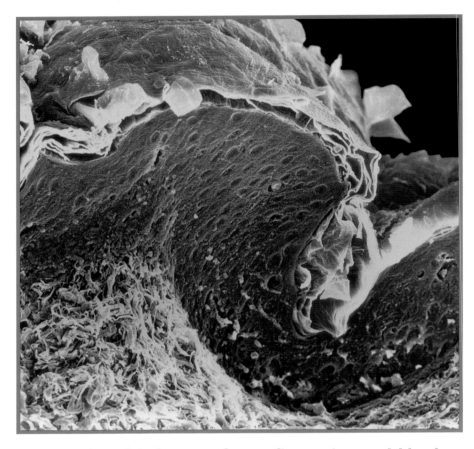

This is what skin layers of your fingertip would look like if you magnified it hundreds of times.

the world around you. Your skin is indeed remarkable, but it can get damaged in various ways.

The skin is made up of billions of tiny cells, each too small to see without a microscope. Actually, the cells in the outer part of your skin are dead. But new skin cells are constantly forming underneath them. They will move outward and eventually die, too. Each skin cell lives an average of only 28 days.

The dead cells on the outside of your skin form a thick, tough protective layer. They are mostly made of a protein called keratin. You may never notice it, but some of the dead cells in this outer keratin layer are continually flaking off.

The keratin layer protects the living cells inside your body. It keeps out disease germs and also keeps body fluids from leaking out.

Just beneath the keratin layer, there are two layers of living skin cells. The top layer is called the epidermis. The epidermis contains the cells that form the keratin

You Lost What?

When you shake someone's hand or wash your hands, you may lose as many as 40,000 dead skin cells in one minute!

Handy Healthy Fact

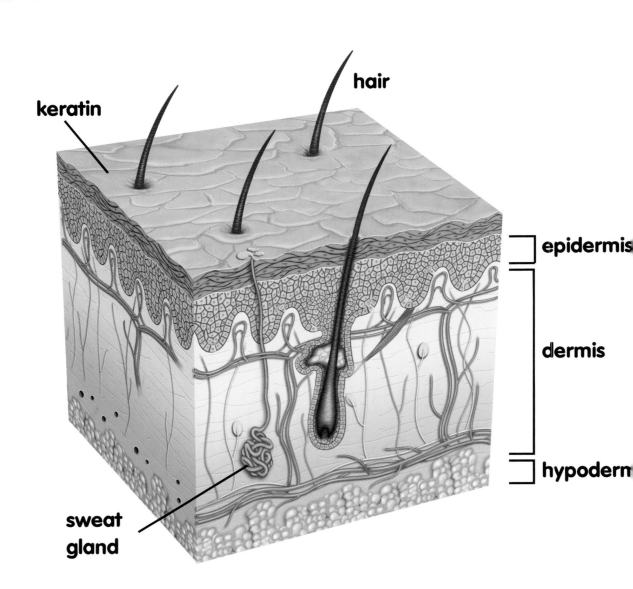

keratin

hair

epidermis

dermis

hypoderm

sweat gland

Here is a close-up look inside the skin. A minor burn affects just the epidermis, but more serious burns affect the dermis and hypodermis, too.

layer when they die. The epidermis is very thin. It is only about as thick as a sheet of paper.

The epidermis lies on top of another layer of living skin cells called the dermis. The dermis makes up about 90 percent of the skin's thickness. The dermis contains nerve endings. Nerves send messages from the dermis to your brain about things you touch or feel. With a single touch, you can tell if an object is rough or smooth, hot or cold. If you touch something that is too hot, or sharp enough to hurt you, nerve endings send pain messages to your brain that may make you say "Ouch!"

Skin cells need food and oxygen to live and grow. These important materials are carried in the blood by millions of tiny blood vessels that are found in the dermis. There are no blood vessels in the epidermis. That's why a shallow scratch doesn't bleed.

3

WHEN YOU GET BURNED

When you burn your skin on a hot stove, skin cells are damaged by the heat. These skin cells send out chemicals that act as alarm signals. They tell the body something is wrong. The alarm chemicals also trigger the surrounding nerves, causing you to feel pain.

Some of these chemicals cause plasma—the clear fluid in blood—to leak out of nearby blood vessels into body tissues, making them swollen. The body tissues also become hot and red. This process is called inflammation.

As the heat kills skin cells, layers of the epidermis and possibly the dermis become separated. Plasma then seeps into the gap and fills it up, causing a bubblelike blister to form.

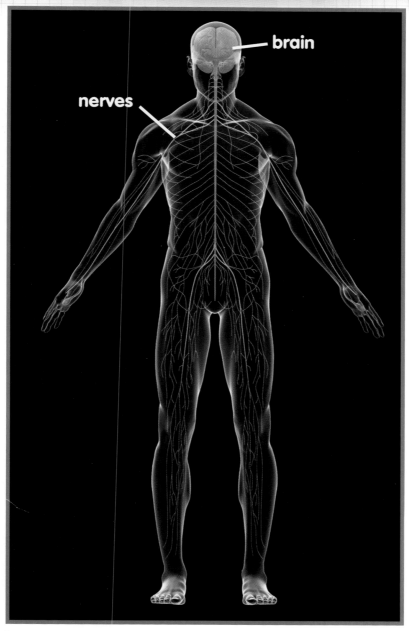

brain

nerves

Your brain controls many parts of your body by sending and receiving messages. Nerves carry those messages to and from the brain.

Mixed Signals

Your body's pain signals can get mixed up sometimes. An ice cube feels "burning hot" because your nerves are triggered by extreme temperatures, which include both hot and cold.

Meanwhile, the damaged blood vessels also release chemicals that send signals. They call in jellylike white blood cells that can move through blood and tissues.

White blood cells can move most easily through inflamed, fluid-filled tissues. They squeeze out of tiny holes in the walls of blood vessels and move through the fluid in the gaps between cells. The white blood cells act like a clean-up squad. When they come into contact with the damaged tissue, they eat up dead cells and bits of dirt in the wound.

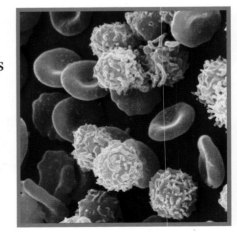

This is what your white and red blood cells would look like if they were magnified over 10,000 times.

What happens next depends on how much damage there is. The body's major job is healing: repairing the damage so that the skin is whole again. In minor burns—those that do not go below the epidermis—the healing process is fairly simple. Skin cells in the tissues around the burn start to multiply. Each cell divides in half to form two smaller skin cells. These new skin

Don't Burst a Blister

Bursting a blister on your skin may seem like fun—like popping the bubbles on a sheet of plastic bubble wrap. But try not to burst the blister from a burn. If you do, bacteria can get inside and cause an infection. Then the burn will take much longer to heal.

A blister actually protects the burn just as a scab protects a cut. Eventually, the damaged tissue underneath the blister heals. The plasma seeps back into the tissues and the blister gets smaller. Finally, the dead part peels off when it is no longer needed for protection.

cells grow quickly and move into the wound area. There they continue to grow and multiply until the gap is filled in with new skin.

Burns can get infected easily because the protective outer layers of skin are gone. Then your body tissues are exposed, making it easier for germs to get inside. If an infection develops, the damaged cells call in white blood cells, which quickly arrive to attack the foreign invaders. They gobble up germs and damaged cells. But germs produce poisons, and after a white blood cell has eaten a lot of them, it dies.

For severe burns—those that are very large or very deep—the healing process is a bit more complicated. Two kinds of cells multiply and move up into the wound: new skin cells and fibroblasts. Fibroblasts form tough threads of protein that build a framework over the damaged area. They also pull the edges of the wound together so that there is a smaller gap to fill. A protein called collagen, made by the fibroblasts, acts as a glue and a support. Both skin cells and fibroblasts multiply, gradually filling in the gap.

The new skin that closes the gap contains a lot of collagen fibers along with epidermis and dermis cells.

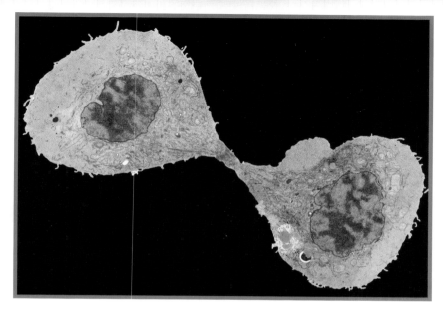

These two cells are almost finished dividing.

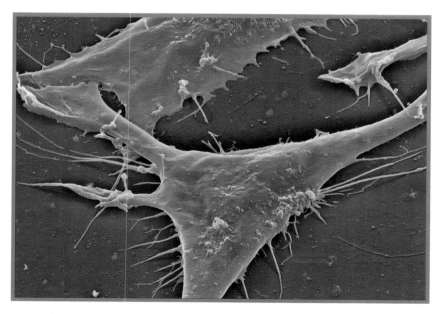

This is what fibroblasts look like magnified thousands of times.

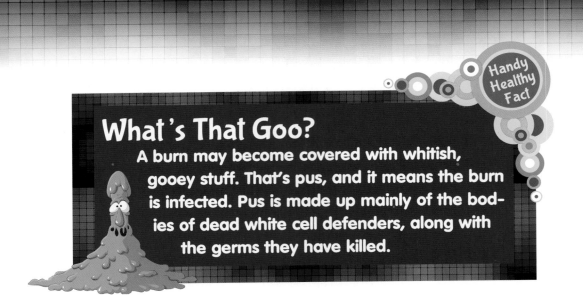

What's That Goo?

A burn may become covered with whitish, gooey stuff. That's pus, and it means the burn is infected. Pus is made up mainly of the bodies of dead white cell defenders, along with the germs they have killed.

The areas of collagen form a scar, which does not look quite like normal skin. It does not have the chemicals that give skin its usual color, and no hair grows out of the scarred area. But the collagen fibers make scar tissue much stronger than normal skin. The size of a burn scar depends on how much tissue was damaged. More collagen is needed to cover a larger gap, so healing leaves a bigger scar.

How long a burn takes to heal depends on how serious the skin damage. Mild burns heal rather quickly, in about one to two weeks, with little or no scarring. More severe burns, however, can take much longer to repair (possibly months or even years) and there is often a lot of scarring.

Scar tissue does the job of closing up a wound and covering the burn tissue with a strong, protective layer. But the collagen fibers are so strong that they may pull the surrounding tissues together too tightly. Scar tissue that forms on a burned hand, for example, may make it hard to move the fingers.

Doctors may be able to prevent scars from developing or repair scar tissue with skin grafts. These are thin layers of skin taken from another part of the body to cover a wound. Artificial tissue, grown in a laboratory, may also be used for skin grafts. The living skin cells in the graft multiply and cover the damaged area with new skin. Then there is no scar. But for people with severe burns, getting rid of scars may not be possible.

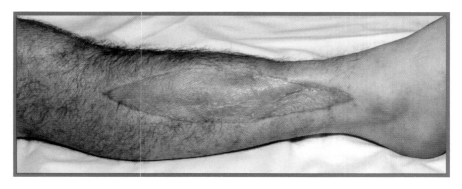

Doctors can use a skin graft to repair a severe burn, preventing the formation of scars.

4

KINDS OF BURNS

Most burns occur at home. A number of different things can burn you. The most common kind of burn is caused by dry heat. You can get this kind of burn from matches, stoves, ovens, irons, heaters, or even a lightbulb.

If you hop into a shower or bath and the water is too hot, you can scald your skin. Scalds are burns that are caused by hot liquids or steam (water in gas form). You can scald the inside of your mouth or throat by

Whenever you take something out of the oven, be sure to use pot holders.

A shower that is too hot can scald your skin.

Hot liquids can scald your tongue.

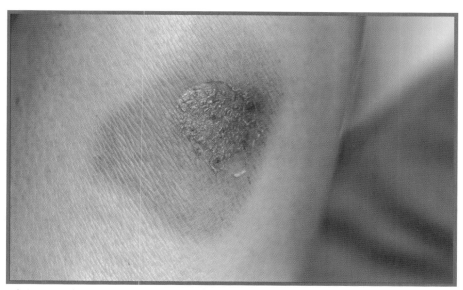

This scald was caused by hot liquid or steam.

Activity 1: What's Rug Burn?

Have you ever tripped while running indoors and gone sliding along the carpet? If you were wearing shorts, you probably wound up with red, hot, painful knees. They weren't exactly like the scraped knees you get when you fall outdoors. The skin wasn't broken and you weren't bleeding. You actually got a burn. Baseball players sometimes get this kind of injury, too. Even though their long pants protect them from scrapes, sliding into a base on a close play can give them a "raspberry" — a painful red patch on the outside of the thigh.

How can you get a burn without touching anything hot? Actually, there was heat involved, and you yourself helped to create it. When you slid, your knees rubbed against the carpet. And when two solids rub against each other, the friction between them generates heat.

You can find out for yourself just how much heat friction can produce. You'll need an indoor-outdoor thermometer—the kind that has a small metal probe attached by a wire. First tape the probe to the palm of your hand with a small piece of sticky tape and leave it in place for a minute (or until the temperature on the thermometer stays steady). Write down that temperature, and then remove the probe and rub the palms of your hands against each other as hard and fast as you can. You'll feel the heat building up between them. Now slip the thermometer probe between your palms and hold them tightly together until you get a steady temperature reading. How many degrees did the friction raise the temperature of your palms?

Your palms are smooth, so the friction between them didn't make enough heat to burn you. But rubbing against the rougher surface of a carpet can give you a mild "rug burn."

drinking a steaming cup of hot chocolate. Or you can scald your hand by touching the steam that comes out of a pot of boiling water.

Certain chemicals can also produce burns. For instance, chlorine bleach or very strong cleaning products can burn your skin. Gasoline can burn you, too.

Electricity can be very dangerous. If you touch a frayed electric cord, you will get a shock that feels like a painful punch. You may also get burned. Even if you don't see any damage to your skin, the electric shock may have caused serious burns inside your body. In this case, go see a doctor.

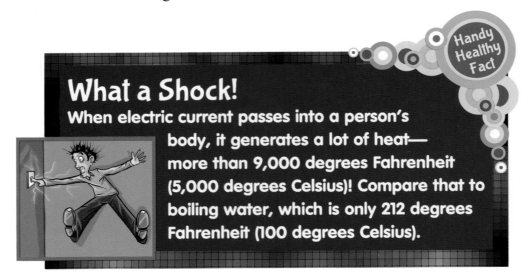

Handy Healthy Fact

What a Shock!
When electric current passes into a person's body, it generates a lot of heat—more than 9,000 degrees Fahrenheit (5,000 degrees Celsius)! Compare that to boiling water, which is only 212 degrees Fahrenheit (100 degrees Celsius).

5

CLASSIFYING BURNS

Doctors separate burns into three categories depending on how serious they are.

A minor burn is called a first-degree burn. The skin is swollen, reddened, and painful. Only the outer layer (the epidermis) is damaged. Briefly touching a hot object, such as a stove or iron, is a common cause of first-degree burns.

A second-degree burn is more serious. It affects both the outer skin layer and the one underneath it (the epidermis and the dermis). Fluid-filled blisters usually develop in second-degree burns.

The most serious type of burn is a third-degree burn. In this case, all the skin layers are destroyed, as are some tissues underneath. The skin may look white, very red,

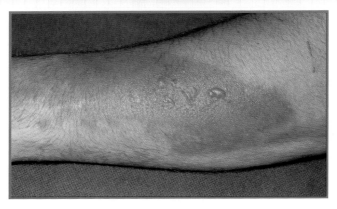

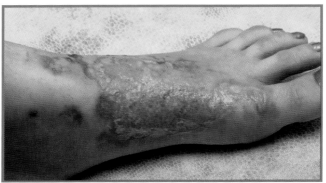

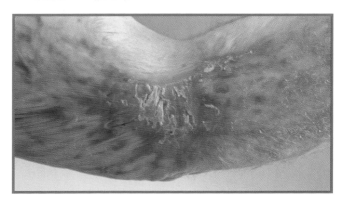

The top photo shows a first degree burn. The middle photo shows a second-degree burn. The bottom photo shows a third-degree burn.

26

or even blackened. Plasma leaks out of the tissues, but blisters do not form because the outer layers of skin are gone. You would think that this kind of burn is extremely painful. Actually, many patients with third-degree burns don't feel any pain at all because the nerve endings have been destroyed. A third-degree burn may need a lot of skin grafting. As the wounds heal, major scars form.

Fire is a common cause of third-degree burns. People who survive fires may be left with burns that cover much of their bodies. When this happens, serious or even life-threatening complications may develop.

Going Into Shock

Severe burns can be very dangerous. The body loses a lot of fluids when it is burned. These fluids are needed to keep the heart and kidneys working properly and to supply the body cells with the oxygen and nutrients they need to function. Lack of these fluids can put a person into shock. Some early signs of shock may include a pale face; cold, sweaty hands and feet; shallow, fast breathing; weak pulse rate; and confusion. Later, the person may be very restless and thirsty, may have trouble breathing, and may possibly lose consciousness. Health workers need to look for signs of shock when they are treating third-degree burn victims.

6

SUNBURN

A day at the beach is a lot of fun on a hot summer day. But if you're not careful, a day of fun in the sun can lead to a very uncomfortable night. Sunburn is one of the most common kinds of burns. The sun sends out harmful ultraviolet rays (UV rays) that can make your skin red and painful when you stay out in it for too long. Sunburn is a warning that UV rays have hurt your skin.

Even though the sunburn eventually goes away, the injury to the skin remains. Some studies show that kids who get sunburned have a higher risk of getting skin cancer as adults.

Sunburn is one of the most common kinds of burns.

Are Tans Healthy?

Some people think that a tan makes you look healthy. But the truth is that when you get a tan, you are actually damaging your skin. Even being exposed to artificial sunlight from a tanning salon can damage your skin in the long run. So basically, there is no such thing as a "safe tan."

Most sunburns are first-degree burns, and they are often very painful. When sunburn covers much of your body, it may be too painful to do your everyday activities—even sleeping.

You can avoid getting sunburned by putting on sunscreen or sunblock. Sunscreen lotion soaks up some of the sun's UV rays, so they never get a chance to hurt your skin. Sunblock keeps *all* of the UV rays from reaching your skin. When you put on sunscreen or

Make sure you use sunscreen or sunblock whenever you are in the sun.

sunblock, you are putting on an invisible suit of armor. The best sunscreens and sunblocks have a sun protection factor (SPF) of 15 or higher. If you sweat a lot or go swimming, though, the water will wash away your protection. So be sure to reapply these lotions frequently.

Does Everybody Get Sunburned?

Anyone can get sunburned—no matter what color their skin is. However, people with light-colored skin burn more easily and more severely than those with dark-colored skin. Human skin contains tiny black grains called melanin that protect us from the sun's harmful rays. Dark skin contains more melanin than light skin, so it can handle more sun. But the protection isn't complete, so dark-skinned people need to use sunscreen or sunblock too.

Be sure to reapply sunscreen every few hours, or more often if you are in the water.

7

TREATING A BURN

Most burns are mild and can be treated at home. For a first-degree burn, the first thing to do is to remove any clothing close to the skin unless it is stuck to the burn. Then quickly run cool water over the burn for eight to fifteen minutes. This will help reduce the pain and swelling. The burn should then be covered with a dry, clean dressing (made of non-stick gauze) to protect it from germs. If the burn wound starts to ooze, see a doctor.

A cool bath can help ease the pain of sunburn. Creams and lotions that are not greasy can

If you burn your hand, make sure you put it under cold water right away.

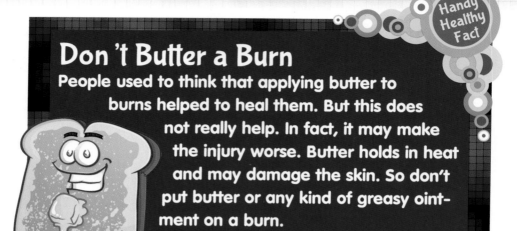

Don't Butter a Burn

People used to think that applying butter to burns helped to heal them. But this does not really help. In fact, it may make the injury worse. Butter holds in heat and may damage the skin. So don't put butter or any kind of greasy ointment on a burn.

also make you more comfortable and help healing. Pain medications, such as acetaminophen or ibuprofen may be helpful, too. Ibuprofen not only eases pain but also reduces swelling and inflammation.

For more serious burns—when blisters develop or the skin is broken, you should see a doctor. The wound must be cleaned thoroughly and wrapped in clean dressings to avoid infection. Sometimes tetanus bacteria may get inside a burn and cause serious trouble.

Tetanus bacteria don't cause too much trouble in shallow wounds, but they multiply quickly in deep cuts or severe burns. If these bacteria spread into your bloodstream, they can cause a condition called lockjaw. Your muscles get so stiff that you can't move. You can't even open your mouth to eat or talk. Tetanus bacteria can sometimes cause death. Babies are given shots to protect them against tetanus, but the protection doesn't last forever. You should get a booster shot every ten years to stay protected.

People with severe burns—those that cover more than 10 percent of the body—should go to the hospital. The doctor must remove the damaged, often blackened

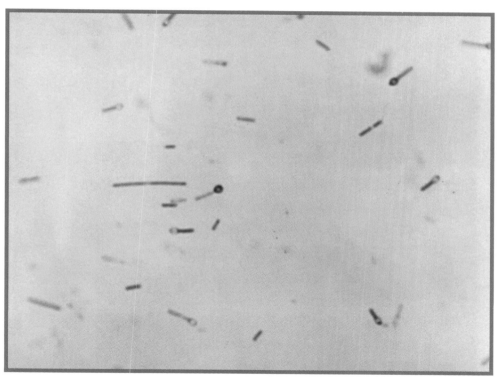

These are tetanus bacteria shown at thousands of times their real size.

Activity 2: Make a Burn Survey

Everybody gets burns. They happen more often to kids, but adults get them, too! Take a look at the examples of burns listed below. How many of them have happened to you?

To find out how common these burns are, you can interview friends and family. First, write down these burn examples on a piece of paper. Then go through the list with each person. Put a check next to all the burns that have happened to the person. Which kinds of burns are most common?

BURN CHECKLIST:
- Hot steam
- Hot shower
- Piping hot slice of pizza
- Sizzling vegetable oil in a frying pan
- Hot stove
- Hot curling iron
- Drinking steaming hot coffee or tea
- A splash of hot coffee on the skin
- Spilled bleach or gasoline onto the skin
- Biting on electrical cords
- Sticking fingers or objects into electrical outlets
- Sunburn
- Rug burn
- Contact with flames

skin quickly so that healthy skin can grow. A skin graft is usually needed to cover the burned area. This is especially true for burns that cover the face, feet, and hands, where severe scarring could limit movement.

A person with severe burns needs to drink a lot of fluids to replace the fluids that were lost. Remember that when you get burned, you lose plasma. The larger the burned area, the more plasma is lost. This can be very dangerous because plasma contains proteins, salts, and other important materials that the body cells need to live. Clear soups and fruit juices help to replace the lost fluids and other materials. If the burns are very serious, the person may need a transfusion. Blood or plasma is dripped into the person's body through a tube with a hollow needle inserted into a blood vessel.

Burn victims also need extra protein and extra calories in their diet, to help fight off infection and grow new tissue. Calories are important because they give your body the energy it needs to heal.

First-Degree Burn	Second-Degree Burn	Third-Degree Burn
Skin is red and hot	Redness, blisters, pain	Skin appears white or black

What you eat is also very important in the healing process. Some vitamins can help burns heal faster:

- Vitamin A helps keep your skin strong.
- Vitamin C helps keep your body's defenses against infection strong, and speed the healing process. Vitamin C is also needed for making collagen.
- Vitamin E helps wounds heal. Applying vitamin E (from a capsule) directly on a burn can help reduce or prevent scarring. (A mineral called selenium helps vitamin E to work.)

Handy Healthy Fact

Eat Up Extra Calories

The average child needs about 2,300 calories every day. A child with burn injuries needs 3,000 or more calories a day.

Foods That Help You Heal

VITAMIN A	VITAMIN C	VITAMIN E	SELENIUM
Broccoli	Cantaloupe	Margarine	Beef
Carrots	Grapefruit	Olives	Chicken
Eggs	Green peppers	Vegetable oil	Eggs
Liver	Lemons	Wheat germ	Fish
Milk	Limes	Whole grains	Shellfish
Sweet potatoes	Oranges		Wheat germ
Yellow squash	Tomatoes		Whole grains
Zucchini			

8

PROTECT YOURSELF

Burns can make you feel miserable. Even a minor burn can really hurt. A severe burn could change your life forever, or even kill you. Fortunately, most burns can be prevented. So what can you do to protect yourself and avoid getting burned in the first place?

You can stay safe by following some important safety rules. Be careful around hot objects, including stoves, irons, curling irons, and radiators. You can't always tell when they're hot just by looking at them. If you help out with the cooking, you should ask an adult to help you with the stove or oven. And if you do ever handle anything hot, always wear protective, fireproof oven mitts. Don't fool around with electrical outlets and never put anything in them, especially your fingers.

Electric hair appliances can get very hot! Be careful not to burn yourself, and never use them near water.

Don't play with electrical appliances and never use them near water. Getting water on a working electric hair dryer, radio, or lamp might cause a short circuit. That could lead to a fire, or give you a bad electric shock.

Do you practice fire safety? Never play with matches or cigarette lighters. Gasoline, chemical cleaning fluids, and starter fluids for outdoor grills can flare up suddenly if there is an open flame or spark somewhere nearby. They should be used only by adults.

How often do you change the batteries in the detectors in your home?

Make sure there are smoke detectors throughout your house, especially near all the bedrooms. Smoke alarms should be checked often. A good way to remember is to test the battery every time you turn your clocks forward in the spring and back in the fall.

Would you know what to do in a fire? You should practice fire drills with your parents so you know what to do in case there's a fire, and find out the safest ways to get out of your house. If your clothes catch fire, do you know what to do? Remember to STOP, DROP, and ROLL. This will put out the fire and save you from further harm. It may even save your life.

Finally, try to stay healthy and fit. A healthy body will heal more quickly if you do get burned. Staying fit will help keep you ready to meet any challenge—even the huge job of rebuilding damaged tissues. That means you need to get enough sleep and regular exercise, as well as eat healthy foods, including plenty of fruits and vegetables. All these things have a very important effect on how you feel and how you heal.

Handy Healthy Fact

Fireworks

Have you ever heard firecrackers go POP and BANG in your neighborhood around the Fourth of July? Sounds like a lot of fun, but firecrackers are not toys. All fireworks—including "harmless" little firecrackers—are dangerous and should be handled only by profes-sionals. When a firecracker explodes, it shoots out burning materials that can start fires and cause serious injuries, such as losing a couple of fingers!

GLOSSARY

bacteria—Germs; single-celled organisms too small to see without a microscope. Some bacteria cause diseases when they get into the body.

blister—A bubblelike lump on the skin that contains a watery liquid called plasma.

blood vessel—A tube that carries blood through the body.

calorie—The unit of measurement of the amount of energy stored in foods.

clot—A jellylike solid formed by blood to close up a wound. When exposed to air, it gets dry and hard.

collagen—A protein that acts as a glue and support for skin and other tissues.

dermis—The inner layer of living skin cells, beneath the epidermis. This layer also contains nerves and blood vessels.

epidermis—The outer layer of living skin cells.

fibroblasts—Fiber-forming cells that make the framework for skin and connective tissues.

first-degree burn—A mild burn; a painful reddening and swelling of the epidermis.

friction—Rubbing of one surface against another.

infection—Invasion of the body by bacteria that multiply and damage tissues.

inflammation—Redness, heat, and swelling that develop when tissues are damaged.

keratin—A protein found in skin, hair, and nails.

melanin—Dark pigment (colored chemical) in the skin.

plasma—The clear fluid in blood.

pus—A whitish substance containing the bodies of dead white blood cells and bacteria.

scald—A burn caused by a hot liquid or steam.

scar—Tough, strong tissue containing collagen fibers, which connects the cut edges of a wound.

second-degree burn—Damage to both the epidermis and dermis that usually involves blistering.

shock—A condition in which a person's organs are not receiving enough oxygen and nutrients to function normally as a result of serious wounds, including burns.

skin graft—A thin layer of healthy skin that is moved from another part of the body to cover a wound so that a scar will not form.

tetanus—A dangerous disease caused by bacteria that can grow only where there is no air, such as deep wounds or severe burns.

third-degree burn—The destruction of the epidermis and dermis extending into deeper tissues. Nerve endings may also be destroyed.

transfusion—Transferring blood or plasma into the blood vessel of a person.

ultraviolet rays—Powerful sun rays that can damage a person's skin.

white blood cells—Jellylike blood cells that can move through tissues and are an important part of the body's defenses. Some white blood cells eat germs and clean up bits of damaged cells and dirt.

LEARN MORE

Books

Chamlin, Sarah A. and E.A. Tremblay. *Living with Skin Conditions*. New York: Facts On File, 2010.

Klosterman, Lorrie. *Skin*. New York : Marshall Cavendish Benchmark, 2009.

Markle, Sandra. *Bad Burns: True Survival Stories*. Minneapolis, Minn.: Lerner Pub., 2011.

Web Sites

Kids Health. org. "Dealing with Burns." <http://kidshealth.org/teen/safety/first_aid/burns_sheet.html>

New York-Presbyterian Hospital. "Burn Safety for Teens and Tweens." <http://www.nyp.org/services/informational-brochures.html>

INDEX